A MONTH'S WORTH
OF
INSTRUCTIONAL POEMS

V Press LC
www.vpresslc.com

V Press LC
Rise Above

Consistently committed to publishing
writing that rises above.

Acknowledgement: "How to Recognize Love When it Has Found You"
has been previously published by Eye Flash Poetry.

ISBN: 978-1-7330488-0-4

PRINTED IN U.S.A.

A Month's Worth of Instructional Poems
© 2020 by Rebecca Bridge

For my loves:
Mike, Baer, and Sara.

In memory of my loves:
Margaret and Billy.

How to Make Butter Like a Pilgrim

Pour a cup of milk into your pocket
and then visit the house of every
human you've ever met and tell them,
*"It was a pleasure knowing you in this
lifetime, hope to see you once more in
the next."* Never look behind you,
just head out West at a slow churn.

This little poem, along with all the others in Rebecca Bridge's *A Month's Worth of Instructional Poems*, seems the product of a marriage between Seneca's wit and brevity and Emily Dickinson's stunning lyricism. From each poem's title to its last word, I found myself in awe of this poet's ability to sustain such freshness of language and imagination, and to hold in perfect balance such profundity and lightness. Though her 'Instructions for How to Be Instructed' suggest we read one poem a day, I dare anyone who opens this book to try to stop at just one.

> —Cathy Smith Bowers, author of *The Collected Poems of Cathy Smith Bowers*, and former North Carolina Poet Laureate.

Bridge's dazzling aphoristic "how-to's" are like the imaginary "hot-cold goodies" I read about as a child in Enid Blyton's *The Faraway Tree*. You pop one in your mouth (or mind) and just when it starts to feel unbearably hot, it turns cold. I've always yearned for someone to tell me "How to Be," but I didn't know I wanted to learn "How to Churn Butter Like a Pilgrim" (nor that it would involve a pocket full of milk) or "How to Be as Self-Possessed as Rainfall." It turns out I do. You will too.

> —Matthea Harvey, author of author of five books of poetry including, *If the Tabloids Are True What Are You?* and a New York Times Notable Book Author.

In a cultural moment obsessed with the possibilities of quick self-improvement, Bridge's *A Month's Worth of Instructional Poems* delivers a truly welcome tonic. These poems pack vastness, wonder, and the simultaneous beauty and tragedy of being both alive and mortal into playful, imperative morsels. These poems won't tell you how to boost your productivity or up your sales quota – thank goodness! Instead, they'll help you simply revel in our shared strangeness and vulnerability. Pay attention.

—Dora Malech, author of *Shore Ordered Ocean*, *Say So*, and *Stet*, and a Ruth Lilly Poetry Fellow.

Special thank you
to early readers including
Isla McKetta, Rodolfo Carboni,
Shana Cleveland and Lakshmi Boyapati.

YOUR MONTHLY CALENDAR

INSTRUCTIONS FOR HOW TO BE
INSTRUCTED:

Read one instructional poem per day
over the duration of a month. Pay
attention. Begin again the next month
and repeat repeat repeat until you can
say with certainty that you've been
properly instructed.

DAY 1

HOW TO REMEMBER LIKE A
BEAR

First set one paw down in the grass.
And now the next one.

DAY 2

HOW TO BE THIN AS A LIE

Don't eat, but when you do eat, don't
swallow, but when you do swallow,
don't enjoy it, but when you do enjoy
it, don't mean anything by it.

DAY 3

HOW TO HANDLE A FORTUNE
COOKIE WHOSE PREDICTION
CUTS YOU TO THE CORE

First, shoot it a dirty look. Next, eat it
whilst you think to yourself, *You
bastard! I hope this hurts.*

DAY 4

HOW TO GIVE HUGS THEY'LL REMEMBER

Realize that your arms are just parentheses and between them there is a word that has no synonym. There is simply the one way of saying it and it means everything.

DAY 5

HOW YOU CAN SAY WHAT YOU REALLY THINK

Understand that words are just little poofs of air husked in a delicate shell of meaning. They will always burst the moment that they are spoken. You cannot change this, you *cannot* change this. Instead, what you can do is remain patient and know that eventually you'll be surrounded by a pile of worddust so thick that you'll be able to doodle your truest beliefs in their word-remains.

DAY 6

HOW TO KNOW WHEN YOUR HAPPINESS IS RIPE

With your index finger, press down gently on the flesh of your forearm. If it's firm to the touch, you're not ready yet. But if your skin gives just a little and then pinks up, you are perfect.

DAY 7

HOW TO TEACH YOURSELF
FORGETFULNESS

Make your mind like a prairie blowing
gently in the breeze and then plant trees
in it.

DAY 8

HOW TO STAY SINGLE

Never, ever allow yourself to go out
into the world when you're looking
particularly wife-faced or wearing
husband-pants.

DAY 9

HOW TO COMMUNICATE WITH THE DEAD

Know that in heaven, no languages are spoken because they've never been needed. Instead, they communicate with a sort of ditting and dahing that's a bit like Morse code, and of course it sounds just like your heartbeat.

DAY 10

HOW TO MAKE BUTTER LIKE A PILGRIM

Pour a cup of milk into your pocket
and then visit the house of every
human you've ever met and tell them,
*"It was a pleasure knowing you in this
lifetime, hope to see you once more in
the next."* Now never look behind you,
just head out West at a slow churn.

DAY 11

HOW TO JUSTIFY LETTING YOUR HEART TELL THE STORY

Sure, it's not adept at developing characters or remembering what happened when and in what order or explaining why it made this narrative choice instead of that one. But your heart's damn good at doing silly voices. And that's something.

DAY 12

HOW TO KNOW THAT IT'S REAL LOVE

If you are keeping someone very close to your heart-ish and they're always in your thought-esques and you don't even care whether that person feels you back deep down in the soul-like, then that's love.

DAY 13

HOW TO SURVIVE A FIRE

Remember that fire is dark; it is not light. Since fire likes to catch you off guard, you must always carry around a personal light source to be safe. This can be a flashlight or light stick, but never candles. To live, you must leave the room before it gets very hot and before 'flashover,' which is when everything around you will ignite. If you cannot do this, goodbye.

DAY 14

WHY WYOMING IS SAFE FOR COWBOYS, BUT NOT FOR YOU

Because in the West there are spaces so open and sprawling that a body may come and then the feet may walk away but a person never really leaves these spaces. Bodies may leave, but other things are left behind and they, too, are so sprawling. So open.

DAY 15

HOW YOU CAN BEGIN YOUR
BIOGRAPHY

Start by blinding every old photograph
you have hanging about. They've always
been able to recognize the lies you tell
and anyhow, they're so preoccupied with
judging who you've grown up to be that
you'll never get far with them staring.
Next, type: "It was a good life."

DAY 16

HOW TO EXPLAIN HUMANS

We are like jars, broken, yet saved for
mending, in still one more container.

DAY 17

HOW TO REMAKE A LIFE WHEN YOUR LOVER HAS LIED TO YOU

Forgiving a liar is like being a just-caught blue crab in a fisher's bucket. Would you rather be one of the poor souls on the bottom who gets crushed to death under the weight of the others, or else at the top where you'll survive long enough to be thrown alive into the dinner pot? Inside that question there is redemption.

DAY 18

HOW TO BE

Be and when you can't be, *give* and
when you can't give, *do* and when you
can't do, *say* and when you can't say,
feel and when you can't feel, *breathe* and
when you can't breathe, *live* and when
you can't live, *vanish away*. It is true that
this is no longer being, but it utilizes a
similar concept.

DAY 19

HOW TO GET YOURSELF INTO A POEM

Walk around shouting "If God had
friends he'd hug you close right now!"
and "Recently the moon has been
coming out afternoons to check on me!"
Somewhere some poet is bound to write
down your words and call you *mine*.

DAY 20

HOW TO DRAW A LIFE-LIKE FIGURE

Check with a handheld mirror under the nose of the figure you want to sketch before you start penciling to be certain the subject is actually what someone would refer to as "alive." If no, choose a different thing as your model.

DAY 21

HOW TO REPAIR A HEART THAT'S IMPLODED

Call the road and tell it to come quick
and pick you up and drive you 500
miles. Have it drop you off at that hotel
you loved as a kid that's now all empty
vending machines and a pool that's been
bricked over. Sit in the bathtub like
a collection of shed hair and soap scum.
Pour water over your head and repeat to
yourself, *This is my home now. This is
my home now. This is home.*

DAY 22

WHY IT'S IMPORTANT TO KNOW YOUR CORRECT SIZE

Someday it will be your turn to shrug death on over your head and it will be easier to settle into it if it fits you properly.

DAY 23

HOW TO PRESS THROUGH WRITER'S BLOCK

Deeply examine the lives of every person around you and concentrate on how not even one of them, anywhere, has a lick of purpose, when you really think about it. That's a human construct. Next, set out to write about every which one and purposefully.

DAY 24

WHY YOU SHOULD LOOK FOR
THE WORLD'S BEAUTY IN
PARADOXES

Because here everyone is the carpenter
and still everyone's the nail.

DAY 25

HOW TO RECOGNIZE LOVE WHEN IT HAS FOUND YOU

When your heart gives you a call, do not let it ring through to voicemail. Pick up the handset immediately and say, *Yes. Yes, I am here.*

DAY 26

HOW TO BE AS SELF-POSSESSED AS RAINFALL

Come whenever you darn well please
and go wherever the heck you want to.
You are the rain and the rain knows that
any and every container will hug its
curves just fantastically.

DAY 27

HOW TO FIGURE OUT WHAT YOU REALLY THINK

Begin by arranging every thought you've ever had into piles, each folded just-so and so very nicely. Now you can sort through the things you've contemplated like a stack of sweaters for sale at a fancy shop.

Remember that you're not obligated to bring anything home with you. You can leave or you can stay a while browsing. In the end, only buy something if it looks good on and you can afford it.

DAY 28

HOW TO RUN FASTER THAN LONELINESS

If you are human, and I suspect that you are, this isn't a talent you'll ever possess because loneliness can howl like a hurricane wind across everything while you aren't capable of much more than plodding about and moving out of the way of things. Instead, sit as still as a traffic sign until someone wanders past and then say, "Stop!" and then say, "Stay!"

Day 29

WHY YOU CAN'T ALLOW YOUR SOUL TO GROW DUSTY

Even a small accumulation of dust settling into an idle soul can cause a 50% drop in performance. Once this happens, a soul's functioning will continue to decrease exponentially. Furthermore, soul dust is insulative, which is the leading cause of loneliness. There are a lot of maladies to suffer in the universe and that's not the one you want.

DAY 30

WHY YOU WILL ALWAYS BE
RECOGNIZABLE

Find a table and squeeze the edge of it
until your fingers turn red and then your
knuckles go white. Keep holding onto it
with every ounce of stubbornness you
have inside of you for at least one hour.
Then let go. Feel how your fingers don't
want to go back to their normal way of
being because they are so familiar now
with being clenched? But then, slowly,
the feeling wears away and you're back
to how you were before you did
anything? That's why it's unlikely you'll
ever be anyone but the you that you are
already. I hope you like her.

DAY 31

HOW TO CHANT SO THAT IT
DOES SOMETHING

Sometime, just even somebody then,
even would I like some somewhat, just
once, once, once with some somewho :‖